T0079977

What's in this book

This book belongs to

_____

你几岁? How old are you?

学习内容 Contents

沟通 Communication

询问年龄
Ask about someone's age

回答年龄
Talk about someone's age

向他人道谢
Thank someone

回应他人道谢
Respond to someone's thanks

生词 New words

★	几岁	how old
★	六岁	six years old
★	他	he, him
★	她	she, her
	我们	we, us
	谢谢	thanks
	不客气	you are welcome

你几岁？   How old are you?

我六岁。   I am six years old.

谢谢。   Thanks.

不客气。   You are welcome.

跨学科学习 Project

制作相簿，并介绍自己
Make a photo album and
introduce yourself

文化 Cultures

中西生日庆祝方式
Birthday celebrations in China
and Western countries

Get ready

1 How often do you visit toy shops?

2 What would you choose for yourself from this toy shop?

3 What do you think Hao Hao will choose?

你几岁？
我六岁。

我喜欢飞机。

你几岁?
我六岁。

她七岁，我们一起玩。

我们都喜欢飞机。

我们六岁吗？
不，我们八岁。

Let's think

1 How old is each child? Match the puzzles.

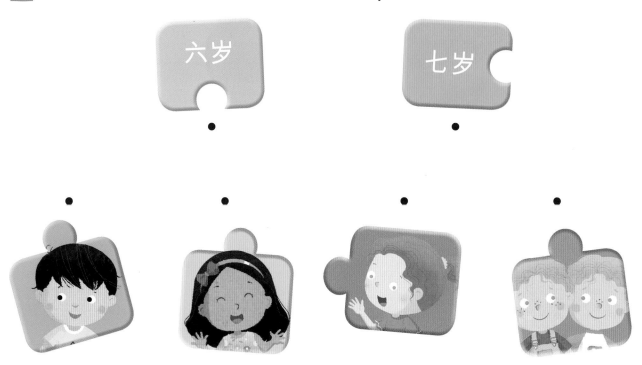

2 Which toy is suitable for you? Tick in the box.

New words

1 Learn the new words.

谢谢。

不客气。

几岁？

我们

他

她

六岁

2 Match the words to the pictures. Write the letters.

1   a 他   b 她   2   a 你几岁？   b 我六岁。

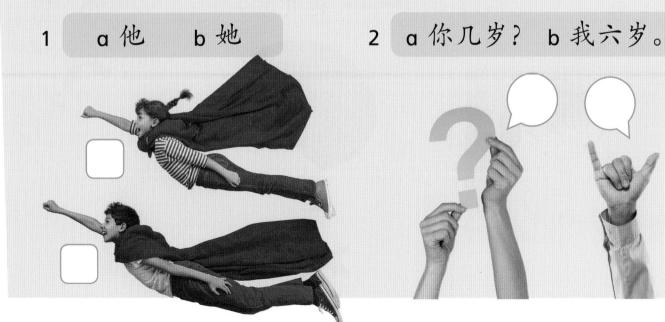

听听说说 Listen and say

03 **1** Listen and tick the correct picture.

04 **2** Look at the pictures. Listen to the stor

四岁 ☐

七岁 ☐

六岁 ☐

1

浩浩，我六岁。
你几岁？

3

她叫什么名字？
她几岁？

2

...nd say.

我六岁。

她叫 Esther。
她七岁。

3 Write the letters. Role-play with your friend.

a 他   b 她   c 几岁

☐叫什么名字？

☐叫 Elsa。

你☐？

我六岁。

☐几岁？

☐六岁。

Task

Draw your friend and introduce him/her.

他/她叫什么名字？

他/她几岁？

Game

Listen to your teacher and colour the birds.

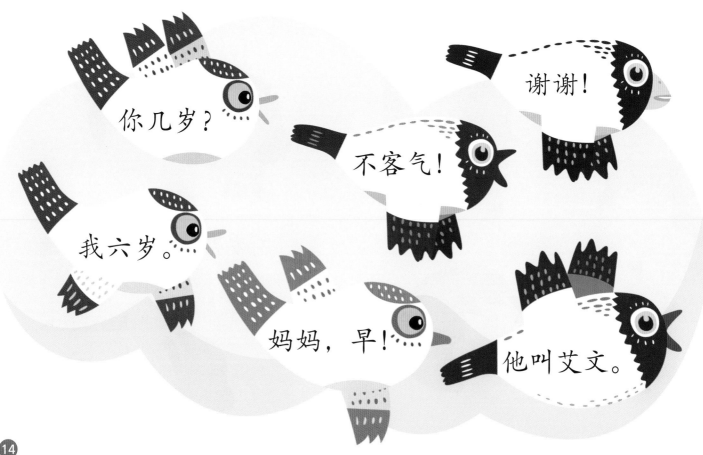

Song

🎧 **Listen and sing.**

我的朋友你几岁？
我六岁呀我六岁。
他们和她们几岁？
他们五岁六岁七岁。

课堂用语 Classroom language

坐下。
Sit down.

站起来。
Stand up.

举手。
Raise your hand.

1 Learn and trace the stroke.

竖折

2 Learn the component. Trace 山 to complete the characters.

岁　岸　岛　岗

3 Colour 山 to climb the mountain.

4 Trace and write the character.

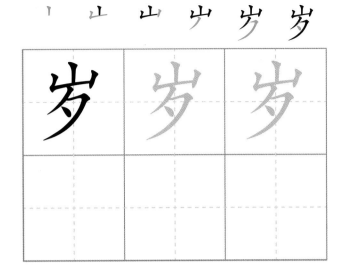

丨 屮 山 屮 岁 岁

岁	岁	岁

5 Write and say.

你几 ⬚ ？

我六 ⬚ 。

汉字小常识 Did you know?

Characters are made up of different components and have different structures.

Colour the components in any colour you like.

艾 颗 十 岁 他 牙

Cultures

1 Do you know the different ways to celebrate birthdays?

Birthday celebrations in China

生日快乐

birthday bun

birthday eggs

birthday noodles

Birthday celebrations in Western countries

Happy Birthday

HAPPY BIRTHDAY

birthday cake with candles

2 How do you celebrate your birthday? Draw on the right.

1 Make a photo album.

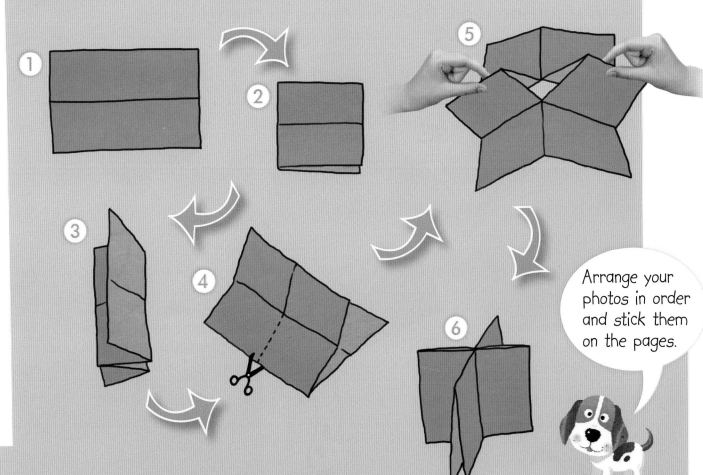

Arrange your photos in order and stick them on the pages.

2 Show the photo album to your friends and talk about yourself.

这是我。
这是一岁的我。
这是两岁的我。
这是三岁的我……

1 Help Hao Hao walk from his home to the toy shop.

Finish

Reply to 谢谢 in Chinese.

Say thanks to Dad in Chinese.

门

2 Work with your friend. Colour the stars and the chillies.

Words and sentences	说	读	写
几岁	☆	☆	🌶
六岁	☆	☆	☆
他	☆	☆	🌶
她	☆	☆	🌶
我们	☆	🌶	🌶
你几岁？	☆	☆	🌶
我六岁。	☆	☆	🌶
谢谢。	☆	🌶	🌶
不客气。	☆	🌶	🌶

Ask about someone's age	☆
Talk about someone's age	☆
Thank someone	☆
Respond to someone's thanks	☆

3 What does your teacher say?

分享 Sharing

Words I remember

几岁	jǐ suì	how old
六岁	liù suì	six years old
他	tā	he, him
她	tā	she, her
我们	wǒ men	we, us
谢谢	xiè xie	thanks
不客气	bù kè qi	you are welcome

Other words

喜欢	xǐ huan	to like
飞机	fēi jī	plane
一起	yī qǐ	together
玩	wán	to play
都	dōu	both, all
不	bù	no, not
是	shì	to be

OXFORD
UNIVERSITY PRESS

Oxford University Press is a department of the University of Oxford.
It furthers the University's objective of excellence in research, scholarship,
and education by publishing worldwide. Oxford is a registered trade mark of
Oxford University Press in the UK and in certain other countries

Published in Hong Kong by
Oxford University Press (China) Limited
39th Floor, One Kowloon, 1 Wang Yuen Street, Kowloon Bay,
Hong Kong

© Oxford University Press (China) Limited 2017

Illustrated by Anne Lee and Wildman

Photographs for reproduction permitted by Dreamstime.com

China National Publications Import & Export (Group) Corporation is an authorized distributor of
Oxford Elementary Chinese.

Please contact content@cnpiec.com.cn or 86-10-65856782

ISBN: 978-0-19-942971-4

10 9 8 7 6 5 4 3 2